FULL SCORE
WSB-12-006

吹奏楽譜 ブラスロック・シリーズ

BRASS ROCK

煙が目にしみる Brass Rock

作曲：Jerome Kern　編曲：宮川成治

楽器編成表

Piccolo
Flutes 1（& *2）
*Oboe
*Bassoon
*E♭ Clarinet
B♭ Clarinet 1
B♭ Clarinet 2
*B♭ Clarinet 3
*Alto Clarinet
Bass Clarinet
Alto Saxophone 1
*Alto Saxophone 2
Tenor Saxophone
Baritone Saxophone

B♭ Trumpet 1
B♭ Trumpet 2
*B♭ Trumpet 3
F Horns 1（& *2）
F Horns 3（& *4）
Trombone 1
Trombone 2
*Trombone 3
Euphonium
Tuba
Electric Bass
（String Bass）

Drums
Percussion 1
...Sus.Cymbal, Wind Chime, Guiro
*Percussion 2
...Triangle, Tambourine
Xylophone
Glockenspiel

Full Score

＊イタリック表記の楽譜はオプション

吹奏楽譜 ブラスロック・シリーズ

煙が目にしみる Brass Rock

曲目解説

コーラスグループ、The Platters（プラターズ）がカヴァーし大ヒットした、恋心を唄った少し切ないナンバー。優しく澄んだサウンドが心に響く、一味違ったブラスロックをお楽しみください。

演奏のポイント

ジャズ・スタンダードとして定着した名バラードを、ダンス・ビートに乗せて軽快にアレンジしました。伴奏のビート感を強調しつつ、美しく魅力的な旋律をたっぷりと表現してください。バスドラムの四つ打ち（4分音符）とベースラインの裏打ちがポイントです。

イントロは特徴的なリフから始まります。最初の4小節間は、伴奏をかなり小さめにしてください。5小節目から「ステレオのボリュームを上げるように」一気に音が増えます。アルトサックス、ホルン、ユーフォニアムのフレーズはメロディーの断片です。Aからが第1主題。メロディーはハーフタイム（2分の2）でテンポを取って、歌うように演奏しましょう。Bからが第2主題です。平行調へ転調していますが、長調になっているのがこの曲の特徴で、魅力の一つでもあります。メロディーと伴奏とのバランスに配慮してください。Cで第1主題に戻ります。ここまでで1コーラスとなります。

Dはイントロと同じ間奏。続くアルトサックスのソロは第2主題の変形です。出来ればPAを使ってください。その場合はトランペット、トロンボーンのミュートは不要です。Eで再び第1主題に戻ってエンディングを迎えます。最後の2小節は唐突に終わるのですが、余韻に浸るようなイメージで自由なテンポで演奏すると良いでしょう。

(by 宮川成治)

編曲者プロフィール / 宮川成治(Seiji Miyagawa)

1972年、神奈川県三浦市生まれ。高校時代に吹奏楽と出会い、音楽人生が始まる。当時は打楽器を担当していた。作曲編曲は独学で、初めて編曲じみた事をしたのは高校3年生の頃だったように記憶している。その後、一般の大学に進むも音楽の楽しさが忘れられず、学生バンドの指導を始め今に至る。

作曲よりも現場のニーズに合わせた編曲をする事が多く、叩き上げで今の技術と知識を身に付けた。現在は学生バンドを指導する傍ら、地域の吹奏楽団・ビッグバンド等で演奏活動を続け、作品を提供している。主な吹奏楽作品に『BRISA LATINA』、『CELEBRATION』、『STAR of LIFE』、『Angels Ladder』、編曲作品多数。第12回「21世紀の吹奏楽"響宴"」入選、出品。

煙が目にしみる Brass Rock

Comp. by Jerome Kern
Arr. by Seiji Miyagawa

Smoke Gets In Your Eyes Brass Rock - 4

Smoke Gets In Your Eyes Brass Rock - 14

ご注文について

ウィンズスコアの商品は全国の楽器店、ならびに書店にてお求めになれますが、店頭でのご購入が困難な場合、当社PC&モバイルサイト・FAX・電話からのご注文で、直接ご購入が可能です。

◎**当社PCサイトでのご注文方法**
http://www.winds-score.com
上記のURLへアクセスし、WEBショップにてご注文ください。

◎**FAXでのご注文方法**
FAX.03-6809-0594
24時間、ご注文を承ります。当社サイトよりFAXご注文用紙をダウンロードし、印刷、ご記入の上ご送信ください。

◎**お電話でのご注文方法**
TEL.0120-713-771
営業時間内に電話いただければ、電話にてご注文を承ります。

◎**モバイルサイトでのご注文方法**
右のQRコードを読み取ってアクセスいただくか、URLを直接ご入力ください。

※この出版物の全部または一部を権利者に無断で複製(コピー)することは、著作権の侵害にあたり、著作権法により罰せられます。

※造本には十分注意しておりますが、万一、落丁・乱丁などの不良品がありましたらお取り替えいたします。また、ご意見・ご感想もホームページより受け付けておりますので、お気軽にお問い合わせください。

Piccolo

煙が目にしみる Brass Rock

Comp. by Jerome Kern
Arr. by Seiji Miyagawa

Flutes 1&2

煙が目にしみる Brass Rock

Comp. by Jerome Kern
Arr. by Seiji Miyagawa

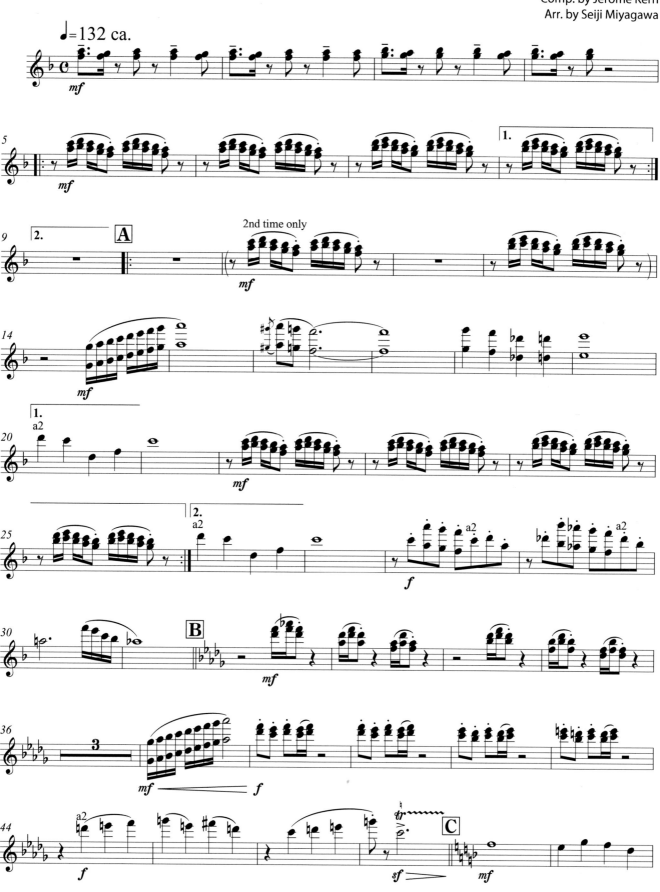

Oboe

煙が目にしみる Brass Rock

Comp. by Jerome Kern
Arr. by Seiji Miyagawa

Oboe

Smoke Gets In Your Eyes Brass Rock - 2

Bassoon

煙が目にしみる Brass Rock

Comp. by Jerome Kern
Arr. by Seiji Miyagawa

05/30

Bassoon

E♭ Clarinet

煙が目にしみる Brass Rock

Comp. by Jerome Kern
Arr. by Seiji Miyagawa

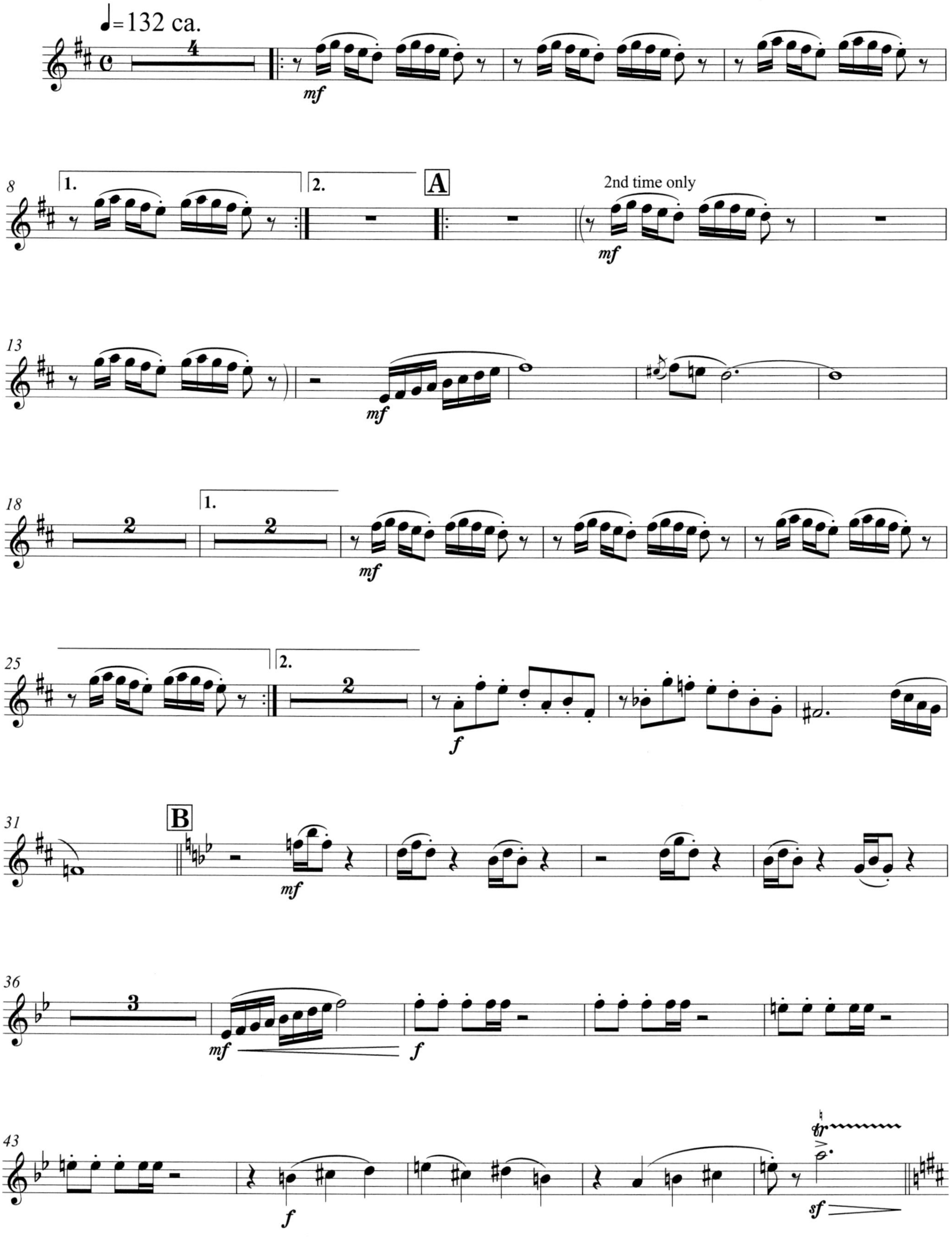

♩=132 ca.

mf

8
1.   2.   **A**   2nd time only
mf

13
mf

18
1.
mf

25
2.
f

31
B
mf

36
mf   *f*

43
f   *sf*

E♭ Clarinet   Smoke Gets In Your Eyes Brass Rock - 2

B♭ Clarinet 1

煙が目にしみる Brass Rock

Comp. by Jerome Kern
Arr. by Seiji Miyagawa

B♭ Clarinet 1

Smoke Gets In Your Eyes Brass Rock - 2

B♭ Clarinet 2

煙が目にしみる Brass Rock

Comp. by Jerome Kern
Arr. by Seiji Miyagawa

B♭ Clarinet 2

Smoke Gets In Your Eyes Brass Rock - 2

B♭ Clarinet 3

煙が目にしみる Brass Rock

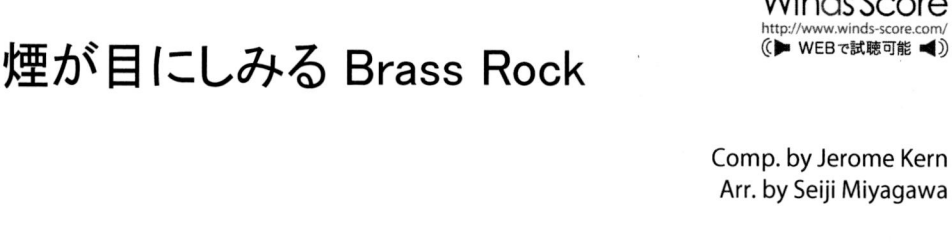

Comp. by Jerome Kern
Arr. by Seiji Miyagawa

B♭ Clarinet 3

Smoke Gets In Your Eyes Brass Rock - 2

Alto Clarinet

煙が目にしみる Brass Rock

Comp. by Jerome Kern
Arr. by Seiji Miyagawa

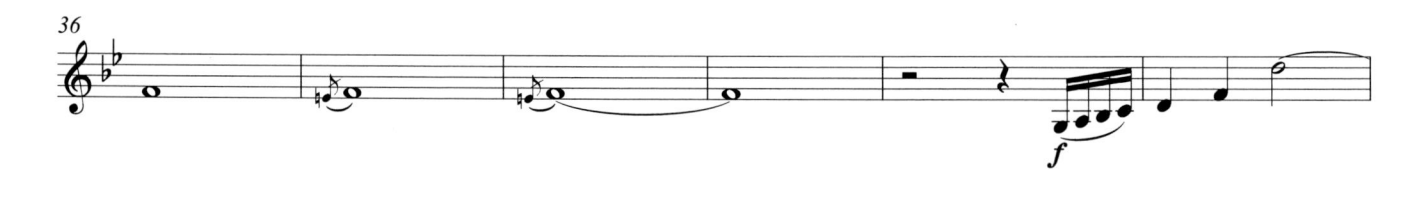

Alto Clarinet   Smoke Gets In Your Eyes Brass Rock - 2

Bass Clarinet

煙が目にしみる Brass Rock

Comp. by Jerome Kern
Arr. by Seiji Miyagawa

Bass Clarinet

Smoke Gets In Your Eyes Brass Rock - 2

Alto Saxophone 1

煙が目にしみる Brass Rock

Comp. by Jerome Kern
Arr. by Seiji Miyagawa

Alto Saxophone 1

Smoke Gets In Your Eyes Brass Rock - 2

Alto Saxophone 2

煙が目にしみる Brass Rock

Comp. by Jerome Kern
Arr. by Seiji Miyagawa

Alto Saxophone 2

Smoke Gets In Your Eyes Brass Rock - 2

Tenor Saxophone

煙が目にしみる Brass Rock

Comp. by Jerome Kern
Arr. by Seiji Miyagawa

Tenor Saxophone

Smoke Gets In Your Eyes Brass Rock - 2

Baritone Saxophone

煙が目にしみる Brass Rock

Comp. by Jerome Kern
Arr. by Seiji Miyagawa

Baritone Saxophone

Smoke Gets In Your Eyes Brass Rock - 2

B♭ Trumpet 1

WindsScore
http://www.winds-score.com/
WEBで試聴可能

煙が目にしみる Brass Rock

Comp. by Jerome Kern
Arr. by Seiji Miyagawa

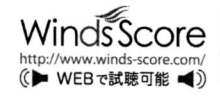

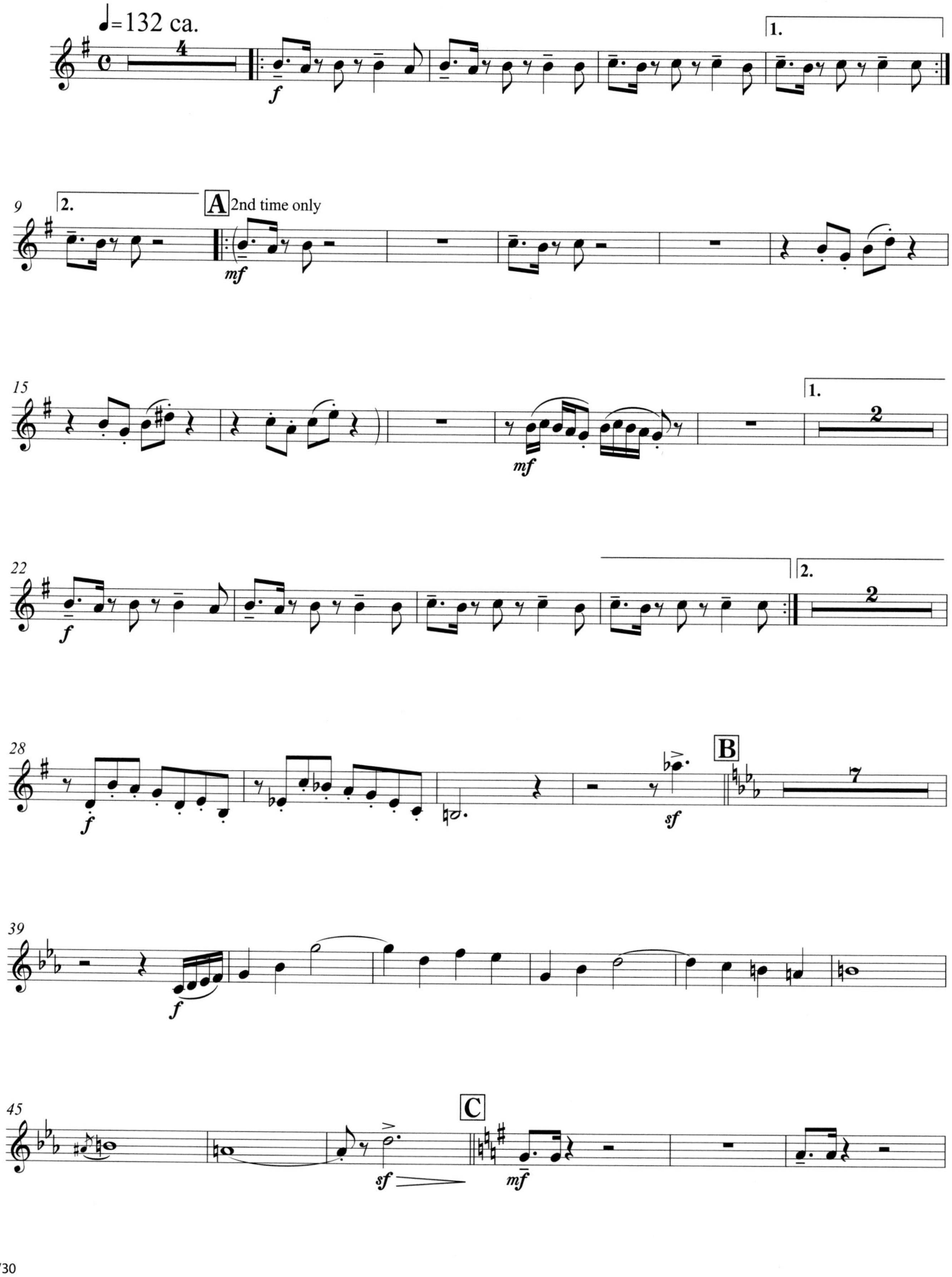

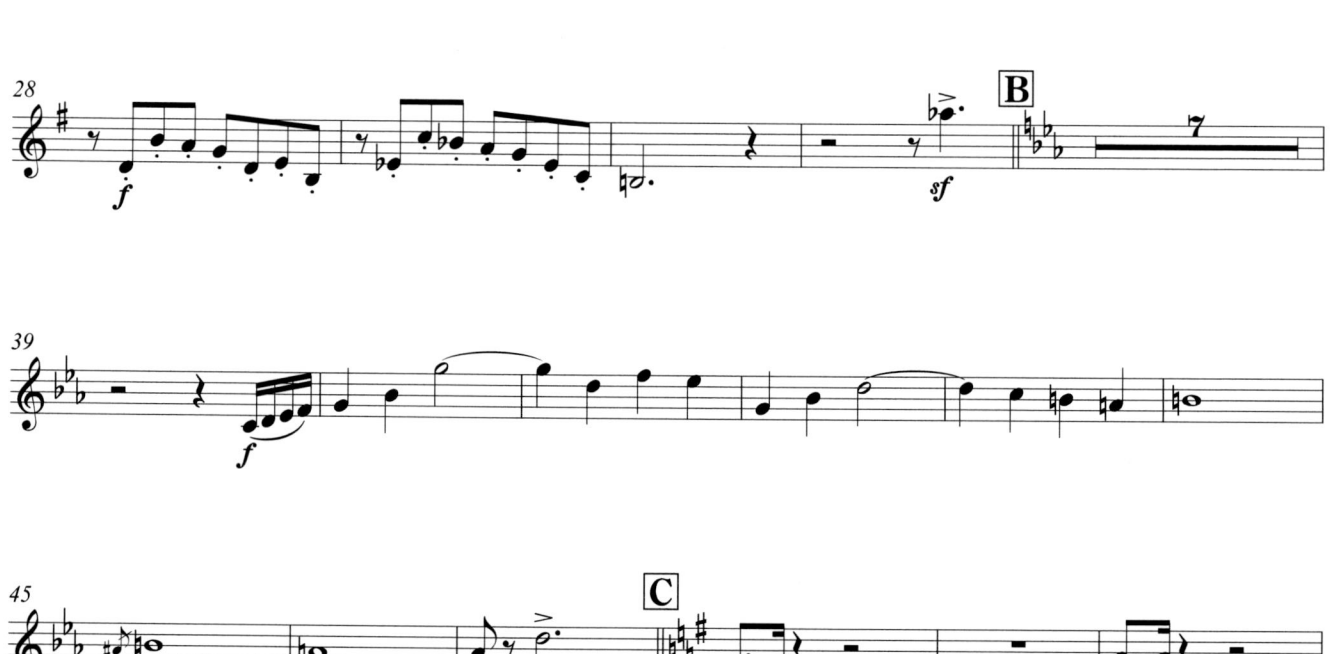

B♭ Trumpet 2

煙が目にしみる Brass Rock

Comp. by Jerome Kern
Arr. by Seiji Miyagawa

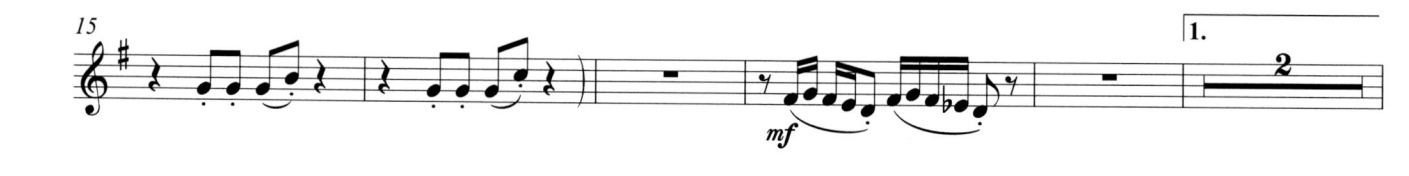

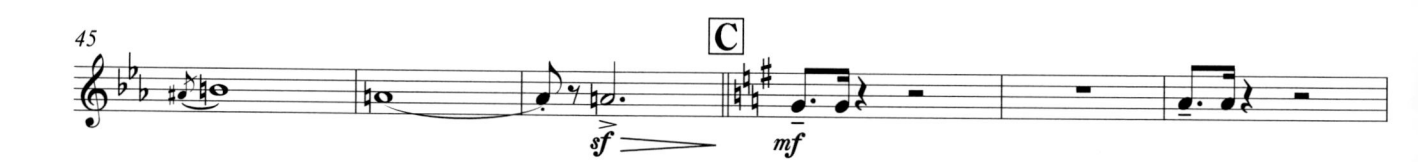

B♭ Trumpet 3

煙が目にしみる Brass Rock

Comp. by Jerome Kern
Arr. by Seiji Miyagawa

Trumpet 3   Smoke Gets In Your Eyes Brass Rock - 2

F Horns 1&2

煙が目にしみる Brass Rock

Comp. by Jerome Kern
Arr. by Seiji Miyagawa

Horns 1&2   Smoke Gets In Your Eyes Brass Rock - 2

F Horns 3&4

煙が目にしみる Brass Rock

Comp. by Jerome Kern
Arr. by Seiji Miyagawa

Trombone 1

煙が目にしみる Brass Rock

Comp. by Jerome Kern
Arr. by Seiji Miyagawa

Trombone 1   Smoke Gets In Your Eyes Brass Rock - 2

Trombone 2

煙が目にしみる Brass Rock

Comp. by Jerome Kern
Arr. by Seiji Miyagawa

Trombone 2   Smoke Gets In Your Eyes Brass Rock - 2

Trombone 3

煙が目にしみる Brass Rock

Comp. by Jerome Kern
Arr. by Seiji Miyagawa

Trombone 3

Smoke Gets In Your Eyes Brass Rock - 2

Euphonium

煙が目にしみる Brass Rock

Comp. by Jerome Kern
Arr. by Seiji Miyagawa

Euphonium

Smoke Gets In Your Eyes Brass Rock - 2

Tuba

煙が目にしみる Brass Rock

Comp. by Jerome Kern
Arr. by Seiji Miyagawa

25/30

Electric Bass Guitar
(String Bass)

煙が目にしみる Brass Rock

Comp. by Jerome Kern
Arr. by Seiji Miyagawa

Electric Bass Guitar
(String Bass)

Smoke Gets In Your Eyes Brass Rock - 2

Drums

煙が目にしみる Brass Rock

Comp. by Jerome Kern
Arr. by Seiji Miyagawa

Drums   Smoke Gets In Your Eyes Brass Rock - 2

Percussion 1
(Sus.Cymbal,Wind Chime,Guiro)

煙が目にしみる Brass Rock

Comp. by Jerome Kern
Arr. by Seiji Miyagawa

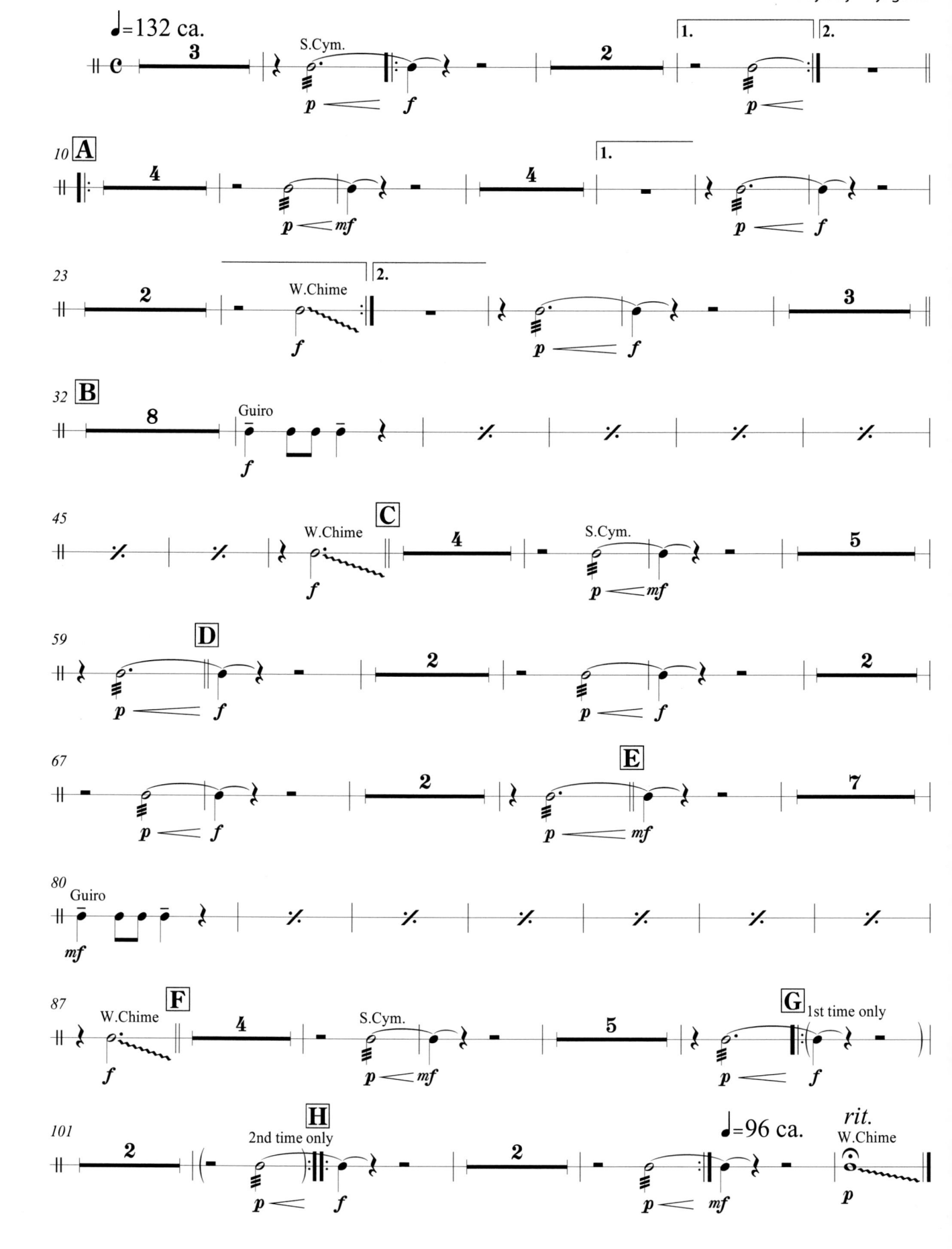

Percussion 2
(Triangle,Tambourine)

煙が目にしみる Brass Rock

Comp. by Jerome Kern
Arr. by Seiji Miyagawa

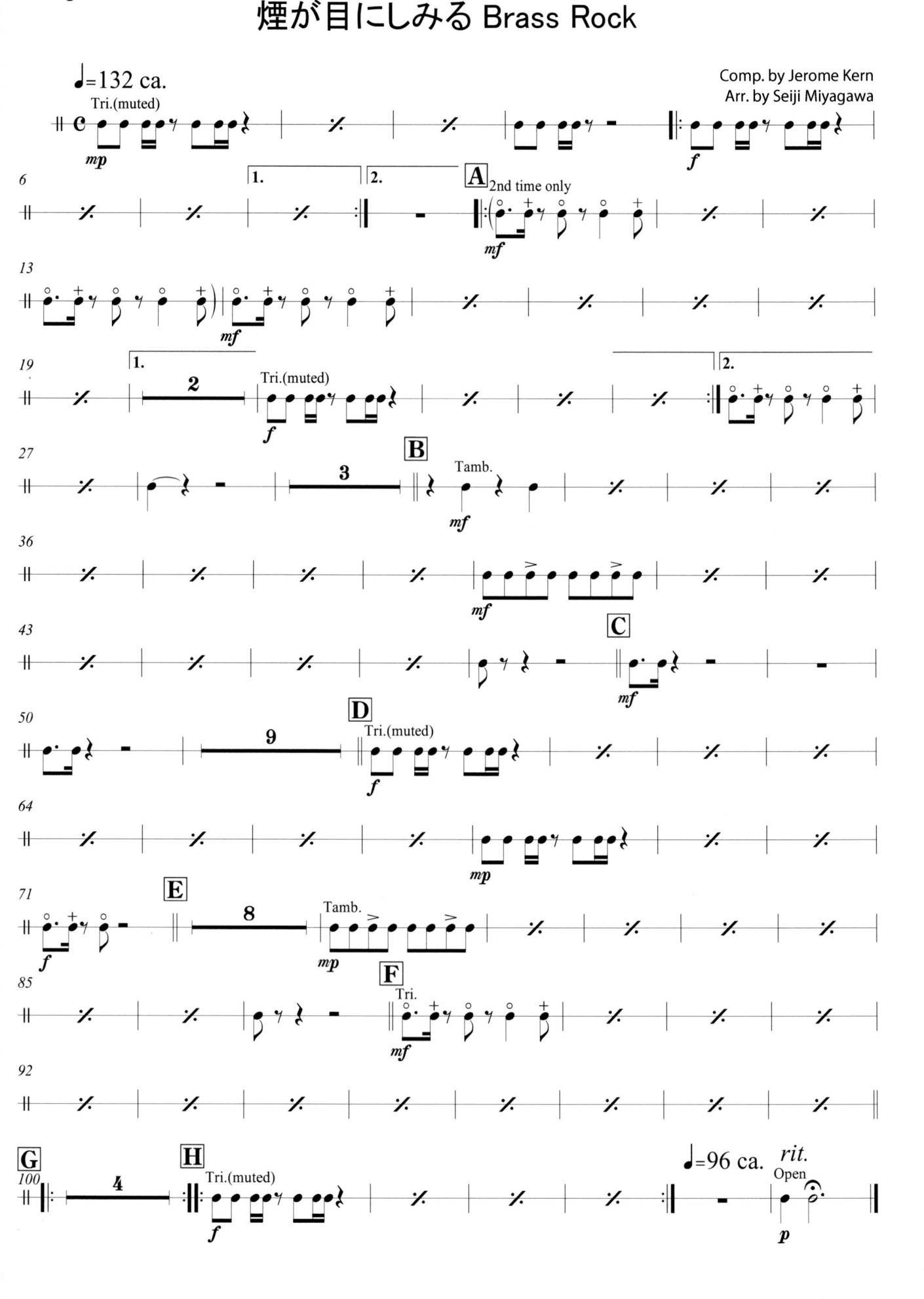

Xylophone

煙が目にしみる Brass Rock

Comp. by Jerome Kern
Arr. by Seiji Miyagawa

Xylophone

Smoke Gets In Your Eyes Brass Rock - 2

Glockenspiel

煙が目にしみる Brass Rock

Comp. by Jerome Kern
Arr. by Seiji Miyagawa

Glockenspiel

Smoke Gets In Your Eyes Brass Rock - 2